Portraits of Edinburgh

by Frank White

Kingsmead

Text by Patrice Sharp

Kingsmead Press
Rosewell House
Kingsmead Square
Bath

ISBN 0 901571 96 2

Text set in 11/13 pt VIP Palatino, printed by photolithography,
and bound in Great Britain at The Pitman Press, Bath

Contents

Edinburgh from Calton Hill

> *"Edina! Scotia's darling seat*
> *All hail thy palaces and towers."*

The most beautiful shopping street in Europe. Paris and Vienna might well question this statement but most Scots would uphold it to the death. Even the depredations of the twentieth century in the shape of Main Street Chain Store blocks can never detract from the rivetingly theatrical backdrop of the skyline from the castle down the Royal Mile to Holyrood, seen across the ravine of the old Nor' Loch, now the Railway.

Holyrood Palace

"Here Stewarts once in glory reign'd
And law for Scotland's weal ordained."

Holyrood Palace, built originally as a guesthouse for the Abbey of Holyrood which was founded in 1128 by David I. In the early 16th century it became the Royal Palace of James IV, but his design was never completed and the building that we see to-day is that of Bruce of Balcaskie for Charles II from 1674–78. The most famous character in its history is Mary, Queen of Scots, during whose brief six years in residence Holyrood buzzed with intrigue and political activity. To-day it is the Official Residence in Scotland of Her Majesty, the Queen.

The Tolbooth, Canongate

"I am a keeper of the law
In some sma' points, altho' not a'."

     Built in 1591 when the Canongate was a separate Burgh outside Edinburgh, this is an early example of multi-purpose building, comprising Council Chamber, Court House and cells below. Beneath its walls passed the tragic last procession of Montrose on his way to the gallows at the Mercat Cross.

Bakehouse Close

"Bannocks o' bear meal
Bannocks o' barley,
Here's to the Highlandman's
Bannocks o' barley."

Bakehouse Close, or Hammermen's Close, was the quarters for these two trades. Acheson House was the residence of the family of that name who were part of the household staff of both James VI and his son, Charles I. With eyes tightly closed and a modicum of imagination one can still smell those appetising bannocks, and oatcakes, and fresh breads and scones which are still so much a speciality of Edinburgh.

John Knox's House

"Oh ye, who are sae guid yoursel'
Sae pious and sae holy,
Ye've nought to do but mark and tell
Your neebours' fauts and folly."

This most memorable of Old Town houses, known as John Knox's house –
that unbending churchman being its most illustrious inhabitant – is probably the
oldest stone building of a domestic nature in Edinburgh.

Frank White 77

Edinburgh Castle from the Lawnmarket

"There, watching high the least alarms
Thy rough, rude fortress gleams afar."

Well known to Festival visitors when thronged with folk hastening to or from the Tattoo. Throughout the year, when the visitors are gone and the scaffolding removed, this is the view that the citizens of Edinburgh still have – the Castle frowning down on all who come to gaze at it.

Advocates Close

"Here Justice, from her native skies
High wields her balance and her rod."

A steep, steep climb from Cockburn Street brings the breathless visitor up to the High Street through Advocates Close, named for a former inhabitant, Sir James Stewart, Lord Advocate of Scotland, who lived here throughout the years of the Restoration, the Revolution and the Union. It is said that the Edinburgh citizen can be distinguished from the visitor by the manner in which the steep Wynds are ascended. The citizen advances upwards steadily and reaches the top unflustered – the visitor runs up the first flight and has to pause, panting, half-way up.

Frank Smith 78

Edinburgh Castle from The Vennel

"The pond'rous wall and massy bar
Grim-rising o'er the rugged rock."

The impregnability of the Castle is emphasised in this view from The Vennel – where the Flodden Wall was hastily built after that numbing defeat in 1513. Pink cobblestones in the Grassmarket below, mark another defeat, where more than a hundred Covenanters died for their beliefs.

Assembly Hall – *New College*

"Some o' you nicely ken the laws
To round the period an' pause
An' with rhetoric clause on clause
To mak' harangues!"

The General Assembly of the Church of Scotland meets here every May, and Edinburgh is thronged with black-garbed ministers and their flowery-hatted wives. New College was built by W. H. Playfair in 1846 as a theological college for the training of ministers in the New Free Church after the Disruption of 1843 when the Reverend Dr. Thomas Chalmers and some 450 other ministers broke away from the General Assembly.

Ramsay Lodge

> *"Yes! there is ane; a Scottish callan!*
> *There's ane; come forrit, honest Allan!*
> *Thou need na jouk behint the hallan*
> *A chiel sae clever."*

The original house, Ramsay Lodge, was built for Allan Ramsay, bookseller, poet and painter, of whom Dr. Johnson said "You will not find a man in whose conversation there is more instruction, more information and more elegance". The crouching figure at the top of the gable which looks like a cat, really represents the Devil, having lost its wings and tail. Originally there was also an Angel on the west gable and a Sphinx on the central gable, all erected in 1894 by Sir Patrick Geddes. They represented the "Riddle of Life".

Franksmite 77

Ramsay Gardens

*"That man to man, the warld o'er
Shall brothers be for a' that."*

Sir Patrick Geddes, biologist, sociologist and town-planner, was responsible for the development in the 1890s of Ramsay Gardens. Professor Henbest Capper designed this unusual group of buildings as Halls of Residence and self-contained flats for the University Faculty. Most are now privately owned, but part is still a hostel for Banking Students.

Frederick Street

"For we are very lucky with a lamp before the door
And Leerie stops to light it as he lights so many more."

The New Town is rich in superb street and house lights – lit by electricity to-day of course, not gas. Gone is the eerie fascination for a child of watching in the gathering dusk for Leerie the Lamplighter with his magic wand that brought forth a blaze of light – an evocation of the long evenings of winter, and memories of blazing fires and hot crumpets for tea.

Heriot Row

> *"Out over the Forth, I look to the north,*
> *But what is the north and its highlands to me."*

Edinburgh, like Rome, is built on seven hills and sometimes it seems that every corner that is turned, every road that is crossed, brings a new slant to a well-known view – such as the green hills of Fife seen over the roofs of Stockbridge and the waters of the Forth. Robert Louis Stevenson lived in one of these elegant town houses further along Heriot Row.

Gloucester Lane

"There Learning with his eagle eyes
Seeks Science in her coy abode."

Craig's geometrically planned New Town took the arts and professions away from the Wynds and Closes of the Old Town. Gloucester Lane to-day is not so very different from the time when Christopher North – the "man of genius" – could be seen rushing from no. 6 to meet another literary deadline, yellow hair flying in the piercing east wind.

Upper Dean Terrace

*"I shall say nothing about the terrible Scottish Sunday . . . 'Let's not go so fast',
said a Scotsman to his French friend, while returning from church; 'people might
think we were just taking a walk'."*

Rising up from the Waters of Leith – whose water was supposed to be highly
therapeutic, the recommended treatment being a long walk followed by tumblers-
ful freshly drawn from the pump – the road curves round into Ann Street which is
possibly the most perfectly preserved street of the whole of the New Town.

Ann Street

"Auld Reekie dings them a' to sticks
For rhyme-inspiring lasses."

This most charming street celebrates one of Auld Reekie's lasses. Ann Street was designed by Sir Henry Raeburn and named in honour of his wife. It was the first street in Edinburgh to have small private gardens in the front of each house.

Frankruile 77

Dean Village

"On goes the river
And out past the mill,
Away down the valley
Away down the hill."

Within the City of Edinburgh still exist several well-defined "villages", of which Dean Village is a fine example. Nestling down by the Water of Leith, almost under Telford's bridge carrying the main road traffic out of the City, it is hard to believe that the west end of the City is only five minutes way. In the late 19th century, founded by J. R. Findlay of The Scotsman, Well Court, a complex of model working class dwellings, was designed by Sydney Mitchell, again under the auspices of Patrick Geddes.

St. George's

> *"Now, God in heaven bless Reekie's town*
> *With plenty, joy and peace!*
> *And may her wealth and fair renown*
> *To latest times increase!"*

The green copper dome of St. George's Church at the west end of Charlotte Square is an outstanding feature of the New Town. Robert Adam's original design in 1791 for a church on this site was discarded as too costly and replaced by Robert Reid's design in 1811. St. George's is now used as an extension to Register House.

Moray Place

"There Architecture's noble pride
Bids elegance and splendour rise."

This part of the first extension to the New Town, planned by Gillespie Graham in 1822, was built on Lord Moray's Drumsheugh Estates, hence his family names being used for many of the streets, places and crescents – Moray Place, Randolph Crescent, Doune Terrace, Ainslie Place.

Drummond Place

"Gray Metropolis of the North."

The Second New Town, planned in 1804 by Robert Reid and William Sibbald, had its main east/west axis along Great King Street, and was a near replica of Craig's original plan. Similarly to George Street with its open space at each end – St. Andrew Square and Charlotte Square – this plan too has Drummond Place in the east and Royal Circus in the west as open spaces at each end.

Frank Smith 77.

Skyline from Inverleith

"*There saw I flouris that fresche were of hew;*
 Baith quhyte and reid most lusty were to seyne,
 And halesome herbis upon stalkis greene;"

When James Rocheid of Inverleith House died, the old Physic Garden was moved plant by plant from Haddington Place to become the nucleus of the now famous Royal Botanic Gardens. From the south side of the house is this magnificent panorama of Edinburgh. The house itself is now the Gallery of Modern Art and the sculpture park on its south lawn includes the works of Henry Moore and Epstein's Risen Christ.

Edinburgh from Salisbury Crags

"Auld Reekie! thou'rt a canty hole
A bield for mony a cauldrife soul
Wha snugly at thine ingle loll
Baith warm and couth."

The finest vantage point from which to see Edinburgh. Salisbury Crags form part of Queens Park, adjoining Holyrood Palace, and how many Cities can boast a 648 acre park in the centre of the city, which contains three lochs, one a bird sanctuary, and an extinct volcano, Arthur's Seat. Each year a service is held on Arthur's Seat at dawn to greet the sunrise on May Day and it is a rejuvenating exercise to ascend this 822 foot hill in complete darkness and to wait, amidst a convivial company, for the rising of the sun. First, tiny shadows of light, no more than a pencil-line can be seen on the Forth, gradually getting stronger, until finally the sun bursts through the mist like a huge rosy iridescent ball, sending a shimmering pathway of reflection right across the Forth.